Augustus C. Schooley

Among the Wolverines

A Series of Letters on the Resources, Growth and Business of the Principal

Towns and Cities of Michigan

Augustus C. Schooley

Among the Wolverines
A Series of Letters on the Resources, Growth and Business of the Principal Towns and Cities of Michigan

ISBN/EAN: 9783337296278

Printed in Europe, USA, Canada, Australia, Japan

Cover: Foto ©Suzi / pixelio.de

More available books at **www.hansebooks.com**

Ever Faithfully Yours
Aug. C. Schooley

AMONG

THE WOLVERINES:

A SERIES OF LETTERS

ON THE RESOURCES, GROWTH AND BUSINESS

OF THE

PRINCIPAL TOWNS AND CITIES

OF

MICHIGAN.

Originally Published in "THE CHICAGO PRICE CURRENT," over the

nom de plume of

MASSABESIC,

WITH AN

ESSAY ON THE CREDIT SYSTEM,

AND THE

COMMERCIAL INDEPENDENCE OF THE NORTHWEST.

By AUG. C. SCHOOLEY.

CHICAGO, ILLINOIS:

CHICAGO PRINTERS' CO-OPERATIVE ASSOCIATION, 164 S. CLARK ST.

1869.

TO THE

TRAVELING SALESMEN

OF CHICAGO,

Through whose effort the Trade of the Great Metropolis of the West has been mainly built up, and is every year becoming more widely diffused, this Little Pamphlet

IS RESPECTFULLY DEDICATED BY THE AUTHOR.

Chicago, March 1st, 1869.

ADVERTISERS' INDEX.

GENERAL INDEX.

AMONG THE WOLVERINES.

[Published in a Series of Letters.]

I.

MICHIGAN, November, 1868.

EDITOR CHICAGO PRICE CURRENT:

One among the number of *voyageurs* who are daily provided with the facilities of comfortable, safe and rapid transportation over the Michigan Central, your correspondent left Chicago on Friday morning, at eight o'clock, and speeding onward through the bracing air, whelmed in the genial sunlight of the loveliest of our Western autumn days, in two hours he was gazing at the sand hills of

MICHIGAN CITY.

Built just where a memorable example in Scripture should have warned its founders not to build, it nevertheless has not yet fallen nor ceased to grow.

The harbor improvement is being prosecuted with considerable energy. Many new and substantial buildings have gone up recently, among them two large and beautiful churches; and the city, in its external aspects generally, exhibits the enterprise and thrift of its hospitable inhabitants. Under yesterday's unclouded sky its streets revived pleasing recollections of the past.

At 7:23 p. m. I took the train, and in an hour was set down at the Tremont House—not the establishment presided over by our genial and patriotic friend, John B. Drake, but a worthy namesake at

BUCHANAN.

Let no traveler be prejudiced by the name of this town, for if the bachelor President did not particularly endear his name to his countrymen, a day's sojourn will convince any one that these people have done much honor to him in naming the town after him. Three thousand inhabitants are here, amid scenes as beautiful as they are busy. One rarely sees so graceful a blending of the ornamental and useful in building a town as is here witnessed. There is a neatness and cleanliness about every store and dwelling that clearly indicates the industry and taste of the people, and the success of all branches of business is shown by the number and substantial character of the buildings recently erected. Through the politeness of Messrs. Ross and Fulton, a young and enterprising banking firm here, I obtained much valuable information respecting the business affairs of the place. May not the general prosperity of the mercantile business here be due to the fact that Chicago is the market whence all their goods come? Nor are manufactures neglected here. The place enjoys the advantage of a good water-power, which drives three flouring mills, a furniture, a sash and door factory, and a turning mill. Altogether, Buchanan is one of the most thrifty towns in Michigan.

II.

Niles, Michigan, November, 1868.

Editor Chicago Price Current:

Ninety-three miles from the Garden City by the Michigan Central Railroad, and twenty-eight miles by river navigation from St. Joseph, on the lake, lies the beautiful little city of Niles.

Like Elgin, Janesville, and others of our Western towns, a river (the rapid and gracefully winding St. Joseph) runs directly through it. On the right or eastern bank is the business part of the city, which is very compactly and substantially built of brick, with here and there a marble front which compares favorably with those of more pretending and much larger cities. In its architecture Niles is not wanting in that quality which is pleasing to the eye, by any means. Just now there is being completed by Dr. Redding, a physician, who has proved to be as well versed in finance as he is in physic, a magnificent hotel, which, when furnished, will have cost not less than one hundred thousand dollars. It is situated on Main street, near the river, and is of its kind the cynosure.

While on the subject of hotels, let me mention the Pike House, built about a year ago, and kept by Mr. H. A. Pike. It is a first-class house in every respect, and delightfully situated on the heights overlooking the city and surrounding country. The view from the Pike House is truly picturesque.

The Bond House has changed hands recently, and, under the management of Mr. H. S. Fay, assisted by the obliging and popular Sam Brown, retains its wonted patronage.

On the left bank of the river, the bluff, which rises abruptly from the water's edge, is dotted all over with charming residences, the most conspicuous of which is owned by Mr. G. A. Colby. It is thought to be one of the finest edifices in the State. G. W. Platt, Esq., has just completed a fine residence on the east side, which adds much to the appearance of that part of the town.

Niles is surrounded by a rich farming district, and thus far her resources have been exclusively agricultural; but being endowed with an inexhaustible hydraulic power, a new race is being constructed, and ere long it is expected that a woolen mill and a paper mill will be in operation. Six flouring mills, grinding five thousand bushels of wheat daily, are now constantly running. The Niles millers have purchased of the new crop of wheat 217,100 bushels, and have manufactured out of the same 41,900 barrels of flour.

Steamers run daily from here to St. Joseph. Gas is just being introduced. The city contains a population of 6,000, publishes two weekly papers, and has seven churches, including two African. There are two private banking houses, but no national bank here. All branches of business seem to be in a healthy condition.

In rambling about the streets one sees abundant evidence of the proximity and influence of Chicago. The architecture is fashioned after the Chicago model. The shrewd, far-seeing merchant perceives the importance of procuring his merchandise of the Chicago jobber, from whom he may order one day and receive his goods the next, and at precisely New York and Boston quotations, in many instances getting a superior article of Western made goods. All classes of business men find in the Chicago papers the most reliable news and market reports. Chicago has imprinted her energetic metropolitan character on all one sees or hears. Even Chicago lager, sweetened with Chicago music, flows in perennial streams; and should you go into a barber's shop, you are offered a Chicago *shave*, which is very grateful to those who know how well Chicago performs that essential art.

III.

MICHIGAN, November, 1868.

EDITOR CHICAGO PRICE CURRENT:

Leaving Niles in all her present glory, radiant with the hopes of a still more glorious future, and being snugly committed to plush, in thirty minutes I was deposited at the sprightly town of

DOWAGIAC,

distant from Chicago one hundred and six miles. It claims a population of 3,000 inhabitants, is well supplied with churches and schools, and publishes a weekly newspaper, the Cass County

Republican, with a circulation of 1,000. The main business part of the place is composed of a compact row of substantial and commodious brick buildings, occupied by experienced and energetic merchants, who seem to be doing a fair amount of business, dull as the times are. Dowagiac has a national bank with a capital of $50,000, and has other banking facilities, amply accommodating her business interests.

From Mr. G. C. Jones I learn that about 100,000 pounds of wool have been shipped from here during the year. The amount of wheat of the new crop marketed here to date is 135,-000 bushels. The mills have made of the same nearly 18,000 barrels of flour. Stocks of dry goods are for the most part pretty full, and were bought mainly in Eastern markets.— Chicago jobbers, make a note of this. Eleven miles toward sunrise brings me to

DECATUR,

which sparkling town is one hundred and seventeen miles from the Queen City of the Lakes, and contains a population of 2,500. The town has three churches, and will soon have the fourth completed, contains an elegant Union School building, and publishes a weekly newspaper, the Van Buren *Republican*, with a circulation of 800. There is a flouring mill here, producing about 200 barrels of flour daily, and rumors are rife that a foundry, which is much needed, is soon to be established. Two new brick stores are to go up in the spring. About 100,-000 bushels of the new crop of wheat have been already marketed here. The surrounding country is highly agricultural, and the best white wheat in Michigan is raised and marketed here. Nor are the environs destitute of scenic beauty. The Lake of the Woods lies just out of town, and is invested with all the romance which its name implies. Mud Lake, though neither euphonious in name nor *clearly* attractive to the eye, nevertheless, it is said, makes a very good skating park in winter, where the youth and beauty of Decatur may and do disport themselves *ad libitum*. Trade here maintains a stolid conservatism. Stocks are fairly up, and look neat and clean.

Perhaps more frequent visits to Chicago by the merchants would tend to convince them that their interests might be promoted by procuring their goods in your market. The trial alone will solve this problem.

PAW-PAW,

one hundred miles from Chicago, at the terminus of a branch of the Michigan Central, is the capital of Van Buren county. The town is situated on the Paw-Paw River, a superb water-privilege, which drives a flouring mill, and flows on in its meandering course through a country of surpassing beauty and richness, till it empties in Lake Michigan at St. Joseph.

Paw-Paw contains a population of about 2,000, has five churches and two weekly newspapers: the *True Northerner* (Republican), with a circulation of 1,000, and the *Van Buren Press* (Democratic), with a circulation of 600. A national bank, with a capital of $50,000, accommodates the business community. The business of the place is carried on by experienced and energetic men, and seems in a prosperous condition, though the dullness which prevades all business affairs in all other towns is also felt here to some extent. Stocks of dry goods do not seem to be in excess for the season, and some orders are being given to Chicago jobbers for replenishing. And now, bidding adieu to the Dyckman House, we embark, and gliding over the Paw-Paw Railroad, in a few minutes arrive at

LAWTON.

It is distant from Chicago one hundred and twenty-five miles, contains a population of 1,000, publishes a newspaper, the Lawton *Gazette*, and is a thrifty and important village. The smelting furnace of the Michigan Central Iron Company here smelts fifteen to twenty tons of ore per day. Gen. Gilmore is President of the Company, and Gen. Grant is one of the stock-holders. The town gave the stockholder 241 majority for President.

IV.

MICHIGAN, November, 1869.

EDITOR CHICAGO PRICE CURRENT:

Fitted out with a pair of willing steeds before a splendid running three-spring wagon, by the enterprising and popular livery men, Messrs. Seymour & High, of Decatur, your correspondent has been for the past week traversing some of the wheat fields of Michigan. Taking a northerly direction from the Central Road, I visited the towns of Keeler, Coloma, Watervliet, Hartford and Lawrence, encountering old friends and a Thanksgiving turkey on the route.

There are complaints of a stagnation in business affairs in all these towns, the alleged causes of which are many and diverse. The failure of the hop crop is the principal difficulty, which is materially assisted by the fall in the price of wheat; and last, though not least, the wretched condition of the roads, which are so bad, so muddy, as to lay a complete embargo on all except that class of irrepressible individuals which is known in the country by the various euphonious titles of "runners," "guerrillas," etc. No depth of mud or snow, no degree of heat or cold, can intimidate these energetic and jolly fellows. Like Alpine hats, they are to be seen every where and at all times. If this system of canvassing the country should be abolished by the jobbing interest, what would become of the hotel business in these towns and villages? Hundreds of thousands of dollars are distributed through the country annually by this class alone; and when all other business is dull, this business attains its highest degree of activity—when other channels for receiving money are closed, this one remains an unfailing resource. It may be annoying to a merchant with a tired brain or a torpid liver to be attacked by half a dozen of these bluff, hungry fellows, immediately after a heavy dinner; but, notwithstanding all this, the system is peculiarly beneficial to him, directly and indirectly. So, messieurs rural storekeepers, we beg your forbearance of our importunities in the future. There are better times coming. Wheat is now advancing, and ere a great while snow will fall, the roads will be passable, and better trade will come. When the wheat begins to move, business must revive, and collections, too, will be possible.

The growing crops are looking finely all through the valley of the Paw-Paw, and the next harvest is likely to be as abundant as the last in this prolific section of the State.

Returning to Decatur from the north, Mr. Seymour harnessed a span of superb blacks, and drove me over to Little Prairie Round, six miles south of the Central, where I saw the Premium Farm of Michigan, owned by a Mr. Hathaway. To those who are versed in ornamental and practical farming a visit to this place is a peculiar delight.

The country through which I drove on this trip seems an almost unbroken chain of farms, studded here and there with growing villages or glittering lakes, or linked together by rippling streams running through them like silver cords, turning the mill and factory, and hurrying on to the great deep, which bears away on its swelling bosom the vessel laden with the products of these eternal fields, to the great marts of trade and commerce of the world.

V.

KALAMAZOO, December, 1868.

EDITOR CHICAGO PRICE CURRENT:

Chief among the towns, cities and villages which form the bright constellation that revolves around and gives to and borrows lustre from the great commercial sun of the Northwest, is justly ranked the *village* of Kalamazoo. Although it possesses every essential feature and characteristic of a city, it has never been incorporated as such, preferring, perhaps, to be the largest village and voting precinct in the United States, to being numbered among the smaller cities of the Union. Whatever the motive may be for remaining nominally a village, and omitting or declining to accept the dignity which her growth and character entitle her to—whether it be modesty or economy, or whether it be mere negligence, it is hard to ascertain. Originally planted in a beautiful forest of burr-oaks, she has rapidly grown in every direction till at present she is more than "out of the woods;" and if we may not call her the "Forest City of Michigan," we may truthfully say, she is the Forest Village of the United States.

Kalamazoo is exactly mid-way between the cities of Detroit and Chicago, being one hundred and forty-two miles from either city by the Michigan Central Railroad. The St. Joseph Valley Railroad, and the Kalamazoo, Allegan and Grand Rapids Railroad, intersect the Central Railroad at this point. The Kalamazoo flows along the eastern limits of the place, beyond which is situated Mount Holyoke Seminary, an institution established within the past two years. On the west the hights are adorned by splendid residences, with terraced gardens. The college is located there, and is surrounded by a grove of young oaks. Elegant church and school edifices are found in all convenient localities. The place is not more a center of enterprise and industry than it is a center of learning. There are two public libraries here. The Young Men's Library contains 2,084 volumes. Its affairs are managed by skillful officers, and are in a flourishing condition. The Ladies' Library has 1,500 volumes. Its finances are in a highly gratifying state, it having at present $2,000 surplus in bank. Mrs. Dr. Stone lectures weekly before the Society, and it is said the proceeds of her lectures have done much to replenish the treasury. This lady was formerly principal of a very popular female seminary here, and on closing the institution last summer, she, accompanied by a number of her graduated pupils, took a voyage to Europe. Since her return she has employed her time and talents in lecturing and writing. She is at present engaged in writing for the *Chicagoan*. Two of her sons are the editors of the *Daily Telegraph*, and her husband, Dr. J. A. B. Stone, is editor of the weekly. The circulation of the daily is now five hundred and fifty; total circulation of daily and weekly editions, two thousand two hundred. The paper is Republican in politics. The Kalamazoo *Gazette* (Democratic) is published weekly, and has attained a circulation of one thousand one hundred.

The growth of Kalamazoo is not less wonderful than that of Chicago. On every business thoroughfare large substantial and beautiful stores are rapidly going up. Among the business blocks recently erected may be mentioned the store of Messrs. Bassett & Bates, wholesale grocers, next to the Kalamazoo House. The building is of Joliet marble, four stories and French roof. On the opposite side of the street was built last year, by Mr. Henry Breese, an elegant store, also of marble, four stories and French roof. Its style of architecture is very chaste, and it is regarded as the finest building of its kind on the street. Kalamazoo is not a manufacturing town, although there are large flour mills, foundries, planing mills, sash factories, an organ factory, and a glove factory here. Its chief resource is agriculture. Perhaps the most expansive and productive wheat fields in the State pay the tribute of their harvest to this market. 650,000 bushels of the new crop of wheat grown in this region have been already received and paid for by the millers and shippers of this point; 430,000 pounds of wool grown in the neighborhood have been purchased by the wool-buyers during the year. The mercantile interests of the place are extensive, and embrace all branches of trade. Some of the largest and best ordered retail dry goods stores in the country are here. Occasionally a stock of goods is found in excess for the present season, and will have to be carried over to the next. This state of things is one of the unavoidable results of purchasing in a far-off market, which renders it impossible to adequately supply a fluctuating demand. Either a scarcity or a superabundance of goods is sure to be, at times, the result of this practice. Generally the latter, as is now the case in many of the towns along the Michigan Central. When merchants buy at a market near them, they lay in as many goods as they think can be sold within a certain short period, calculating that no decline in price will be likely to occur the while; and when such supply is exhausted, they repeat the operation, taking care not to exceed certain limits. A personal visit may be made to the market, where they may select their goods, have them shipped and promptly delivered,—and all at a trifling expense. In this way they may supply the most fickle demand; never experiencing a scarcity, never suffering from a surplus. Their stocks *must* be in exact proportion to the demand; besides, a great impetus will be given to trade by the spectacle of constantly opening new goods, which their establishments will almost daily present to their customers. But the experience of every merchant who procures his goods in a foreign market will compel him to acknowledge that when he goes to that market it will not pay him for the trip to buy goods for a fortnight's trade only: hence he selects a stock which he calculates will last him for three months or longer — often being induced to buy on four months' time, in excess of his original intentions, and waits from ten to fifteen days for the arrival of his goods. Then if, as during the present season, trade drops off, his shelves and counters groan under the weight of an over-stock, which, after the four months have elapsed, begins to *increase in cost*, and from the moment received into his store begins to *decrease in value!* To the reckless operator — the speculator — this argument will have no force; for it is his legitimate business to take great risks, with the expectation of making great profits; but the prudent, solid, thinking mercantile men of Michigan will ponder these propositions, and ultimately must accept them as true.

And now to Kalamazoo, with her ten thousand inhabitants, her generous hospitality, her marvelous enterprise, her charming avenues, and her magnificent views, I bid adieu.

VI.

MICHIGAN, December, 1868.

EDITOR CHICAGO PRICE CURRENT:

Twenty-eight miles down the St. Joseph Valley Railroad, south from Kalamazoo, and twelve miles north of White Pigeon, is Three Rivers. This may seem an ungrammatical sentence at first thought, but the fact is strictly thus: There is Three

Rivers, and there *are* three rivers, viz.: the St. Joseph, the Portage, and the Rocky. They here form their confluence, and give their plural name to the large, beautiful and growing town which spreads along their banks. The stream formed by this concurrence of water is called the St. Joseph, which winds its way through the fertile fields of this part of Michigan, pays a short but "sweet" visit to Indiana, receiving reinforcements from streamlets here and there, then sweeps around into the State again in the region of South Bend, and flows on in a northerly direction till it falls into the lake.

The town of Three Rivers is about 170 miles from Chicago, contains a population of 4,000, four churches, one of them—the Methodist Episcopal—a splendid edifice, just completed, costing $30,000; a Union school, three flouring mills, two foundries, a paper mill, a pump factory, and an incorporated Manufacturing Company, which manufactures agricultural implements. The hydraulic power is unlimited, and the town must eventually resound with the hum of the spindle and the click of the loom. There is a national bank and a private banking house here, each doing a prosperous business, and affording ample facilities to the business community. The Three Rivers *Reporter*, a Republican weekly, with a circulation of 1,272, is the only paper published here. A visit to the office from which it is issued afforded me a degree of gratification never experienced in any printing establishment before. For the first time in my life I stood in a printing office where perfect order reigns, instead of perfect chaos. Mr. Chute is a business man. "Neatness and dispatch" are terms which to him have a meaning. His establishment is a model one, and the character of his work is in harmony with the general appearance of his office. To him I am indebted for valuable information, and for a splendid view of the town.

There is a vast amount of business transacted here. The mercantile business is in the hands of experienced dealers, and success attends them. Stocks of dry goods are pretty full. Some orders for "sorting up," however, are being sent to Chicago jobbers occasionally. The hotel accommodations are good. The surroundings are fertile, and it is said to be the richest mint-growing region anywhere in the country. The oil is one of the chief resources of the farmers hereabout. Running back to Kalamazoo, and connecting with the Kalamazoo, Allegan and Grand Rapids Railroad, a run of twenty-five miles north brought me to

ALLEGAN,

the present terminus of the road. It was opened to this place on Thanksgiving Day, which made the Alleganders pitch into their turkeys with extraordinary gusto. The town is a beauty. It is " among the pines," on the banks of the Kalamazoo, at the head of navigation, and its surroundings are wild, woody, and picturesque. Its chief resource is its lumber interests. The population is 2,500 ; there are five lumber mills, three flouring mills, an axe factory, a foundry, planing mills, sash, blind and door factories, five churches and a Union school in the place. No better water-power exists in the State. Allegan is the county seat of Allegan county. Some five brick stores have recently been erected, one of them belongs to, and is occupied by, Mr. T. C. Jenner, one of the pioneers who commenced with the shovel and pick on the race here, years ago, and has wrought out a comfortable fortune. His establishment is a model of neatness and convenience.

Two weekly newspapers are published here. The lumber manufactured is chiefly marketed in Chicago. Deer abound in the surrounding forests, and sport-men are here from far and near. After snow falls and sleighing comes, then comes the busy season with Allegan.

Ten miles ride southward brings me to

OTSEGO,

which town has a population of 1,000. It is situated on the Kalamazoo river, has four churches, a Union school, four flouring-mills, a woolen factory, a tannery, two foundries, and a steam planing mill. The town is growing ; the country about is highly cultivated. A weekly paper, the Otsego *Herald*, is

published here. Stocks of goods are in good condition for the
times.

Three miles by bobsled conveyance and I am in

PLAINWELL,

which, like a mushroom, has grown up almost in a single night.
About 150 new buildings have been put up in twelve months.
The population at present is 1,500 ; two elevators are erected, a
furnace is building, planing mills are operating, and sash and
pump factories are turning out their products. There are two
flouring mills, two churches, and a graded school. The Kalamazoo flows placidly through the town. The surroundings are of the
richest and most beautiful farms of Michigan. The place already
enjoys the benefit of one railroad, and will soon have another
in operation, as it is all graded and ready for the track. Stocks
of dry goods are light, with an active trade. Plainwell is
receiving many of her goods from your market.

VII.

MICHIGAN, December, 1868.

EDITOR CHICAGO PRICE CURRENT :

One hour's ride eastward from Kalamazoo, on the peerless
Central, and I am in the city of

BATTLE CREEK.

It is one hundred and sixty-four miles from Chicago, on the
banks of the Kalamazoo River and Battle Creek—a stream of
historic fame—which, at this point, proffer their resources to
the miller and the manufacturer. The stone, the spindle and
the shuttle make the music which here fills the ear from morn
till night. Every part of the city seems pulsating with industry,
the life current of prosperity and development. With her
splendid surroundings and her internal mechanical forces, her
enterprise, her energy and her intelligence, she must be in the
future what she has been in the past, one of the brightest stars

in the galaxy of Western towns, and she is none the less progressive in her industry than she is in her ideas, four hundred and eighty majority for Gen. Grant bearing testimony to her patriotism and to her desire for peace. During the Presidential campaign one of the largest mass meetings held in this State took place here. Our galiant Governor was one of the speakers on that occasion, and made, as he always does, a great speech. The people of Battle Creek can appreciate an eloquent address, and they propose to give the Governor a substantial token of their appreciation of his services to them at that time. Accordingly, a silver ice pitcher, tray and goblets of the most exquisite workmanship have been procured, and, ere this will appear to the public, will be presented to him. On the pitcher is this inscription,

"GOV. R. J. OGLESBY,

CAMPAIGN SPEECH GIFT

From his friends at Battle Creek, Michigan,
August 24th, 1868."

On the tray is the family name of

"OGLESBY,"

and on the goblets the monogram

"R. J. O."

The whole is beautifully executed, and is the work of one of our best Chicago establishments. Let the people of Illinois look to it that Michigan does not outdo them in appreciation of our heroic Executive.

Battle Creek has a population of 7,000, has two weekly newspapers, the *Journal*, Republican, and the *Constitutional Union*, Democratic. There is also a religious paper published, called *The Herald and Review*. It is devoted to the propagation of Adventist doctrines. There is a water cure here, which publishes the *Health Reformer*, monthly. This paper is also under the auspices of the Adventists.

The city is well supplied with churches and schools. Messrs. Burrell & Eldred are just completing a splendid block of stores, one hundred feet deep, twenty-four feet front and three stories high, with marble columns. The Battle Creek *Journal* office is now removing to the third story of this block, where it will have greatly improved quarters. Messrs. Pettee & Howe, dry goods merchants, will occupy one of these stores on January 1st, 1869. When the fixtures are in, it will probably be the finest establishment of the kind in the place.

A. C. Hamlin, banker, is building a new and magnificent hall, at a cost of $30,000. The block is three stories, with French roof. It is nearly completed, and when done it will be an ornament to the city. Were it in Chicago or Detroit, it would be dignified by the name of Opera House. The city has a steam fire engine, housed in a beautiful building. The celebrated "Vibrator" threshing machines are manufactured here. A national bank, with a capital of $100,000, established in 1865, is doing a prosperous business.

The mercantile business is not overdone. Stocks seem to be quite full, but probably not in excess. The dealers are moving cautiously, and, of course, wisely. More intimate relations with the Chicago market might be of advantage to them, as it would enable them to buy often and run their business on less capital, besides being in constant receipt of fresh goods.

If the taverniers on the Michigan Central would buy some coffee and give it to their guests, instead of the dirty, warm water, flavored with a kindred essence, I feel authorized by the traveling public to say, that the aforesaid peregrinators would certainly appreciate the f(l)avor. "A word to the wise *is as good as a feast.*" Also, let me remind them that tariff begins with T.

As it snowed the entire time I was in Battle Creek, I am unable to say much of the general appearance of the place, or of the *personnel*—save in a few instances—of its inhabitants, but a glimpse, now and then, between the whirling snow flakes, revealed features which, since the creation of Adam's wife, have solely and exclusively belonged to pretty girls, and from the number of gay turnouts which I saw under the same disadvantge,

"Like me ears flash by,"

during those terribly cold and stormy days, I suspect that Battle Creek is not at all wanting in gallant young men.

VIII.

MICHIGAN, December, 1868.

EDITOR CHICAGO PRICE CURRENT:

Twenty minutes' skating over the icy rails, with the thermometer 10 degrees below zero, and the whistle announces that you are entering the delightful town of

MARSHALL,

which at 3 o'clock P. M. presents a gorgeous winter scene. Windows grotesquely frosted by stern old Winter's artistic hand supersede the curtain and the blind, and shut out from your gaze the gay sleigh-riders who are making the frigid air resound with their merry music ; and

"Oh! the snow ; the beautiful snow!"

it clings in Alpine splendor to the evergreens that deck the yards of the stately mansions here and there, as if it never would relax its cold embrace. A frozen nose, an ear, a finger or a toe, is not enough to placate the wrath of the ruthless monarch, Winter; and since with overwhelming force he has overtaken the few retreating stragglers of Autumn, his war upon them is marked by a cruelty that seeks to hide itself, and mocks its ruined victims by arraying them in robes of royal magnificence. The trophies of his triumph are erected everywhere. He flings his white robe upon the lap of earth, and sits in state upon his crystal throne. His breath hushes the ripple of the lake, and hangs his mirror upon its bosom. He paints his portrait on the window, and writes his signature upon the winding stream. The garnished ruin, the robe, the throne, the mirror, the portrait and the signature to-day make Marshall a scene of Arctic grandeur.

Youth, beauty, refinement, taste, wealth, luxury, activity and success, add to the charms of the place. Six thousand people

2

grouped together in a social community engaged in every pursuit in life, give a civic character to all one sees and hears Fashionable costumes and polished manners are the results of civilization and progress, and Marshall is not wanting in these. Public enterprise spreads her intrepid wings over the town, and a new railroad to Greenville on the north is to be constructed. The road will be called the Jonesville, Marshall and Grand River Railroad.

There are two weekly papers published here. A female seminary under Episcopalian auspices, and called Perrin Institute, is established, and has pupils from all parts of the country. The town has an excellent water privilege, and mills and factories exist in abundance. There are two public halls, the Academy of Music, and Eagle Hall, and two national banks. It is a "red hot" Democratic town, and gave the "astute statesman" and "Farmer of Deerfield" a majority of one hundred in the recent election.

Eleven miles further eastward is

ALBION,

a town of both classic name and fame for D. D.'s and Professors and students, and I suppose learning abounds here. The population is 3,500. The Kalamazoo river flows through the place, and furnishes a good water power. There are three flouring mills, a foundry, and machine shops here. Two papers are published weekly. A hotel, 60 by 150 feet, and four stories high, is about to be erected. A large Town Hall and other buildings are projected. There is one national banking institution here. The principal business street presents a fine show of substantial brick stores, chastely ornamented with mouldings and cornices.

The surrounding country is rich in agricultural resources, and in developing these Albion must continue on in her career of prosperity and happiness.

IX.

MICHIGAN, December, 1868.

EDITOR CHICAGO PRICE CURRENT:

An hour's ride down the Grand River Valley Railroad, in agreeable company, through scenes varied and beautiful, deriving additional charms from a brilliant winter sun, and an exhilarating atmosphere, and I am set down at the town of

EATON RAPIDS.

On the Fourth of July last the whistle of the locomotive awoke the citizens from their dreams of isolation and seclusion ; the bell of the iron horse tolled the death-knell of the stage-coach era, and Eaton Rapids rejoiced in the doubly auspicious return of the day that ushered in a nation's birth and bound them to the civilized world by railroad *ties* and iron bands. The advent of a railroad is the dawning of the highest civilization, and henceforward these people will move on that higher plane, and their activity will be intensified. With 1,600 inhabitants churches, schools, and other moral, mental and physical forces, she will push her industrial and commercial resources to a speedy development. Enjoying the combined water powers of Grand River and Springbrook, she must eventually become a manufacturing center. Already two flouring mills, four lumber mills, a custom woolen mill, and an axe factory, are in operation. Two large brick stores and seventy-five dwellings have been put up during the year. There are two good hotels in the place, and the traveler will find himself well cared for in either of them. There is a Masonic lodge and chapter, and two Good Templar lodges in the town. Thus it will be seen there are warm hearts and cold water in great abundance here, but I must bid them adieu, and betake myself to the road again, where I seat myself in one of the new and comfortable coaches of the G. R. V. R. R., the gentlemanly Mr. O. F. Hall, conductor, and, in a few moments, am off for

CHARLOTTE,

a female, not of the *genus homo*, but of the *genus* town. She is stately, symmetrical, beautiful, growing luxuriantly, instinct with industry, and breathing the pure prairie air. Clumps of leafless burr oaks are standing here and there in her limits, as if counseling together what to do to escape the ruthless axe which has decimated them from year to year. It is to be hoped that a growing sentiment in accord with the pathos of " Wood man, spare that tree," will yet save them from the cruel fate of their comrades.

Charlotte is thirty-six miles from her connection with the Central at Jackson, and will be, for a few brief days, the terminus of the road. Since September she has been a member of the great family of railroad towns. She is no foolish virgin, and her kerosene lamps have been kept " trimmed and burning." Her outskirts are clean and spotless, and she is no " whited sepulchre," for with such choice spirits as John Morris, agent of the G. R. V. R. R., Wm. Benjamin, proprietor of the Phœnix House, by whom I advise all strangers to be " taken in," Sherwood, Hazlett, Saunders, and so on *ad infinitum*, hospitality is an instinct, and politeness an impulse of the heart. Then there are ladies, too, whose names I have not forgotten, yet forbear to print, but for whose presence Charlotte, with all her natural and artificial charms, might be

" Unloved, unhonored and unsung."

The population is modestly estimated at 2,500, but a magnificent frescoed public hall, 50 by 100 in dimensions, a lecture association and other kindred institutions, having for their object mental and moral culture, would seem to indicate double that number of inhabitants. The stamp of cultivated taste is visible everywhere. The ornamental and the useful have wrought hand in hand on the stately dwelling and the massive ware house. Such dry goods establishments as Messrs. E. and J. Shepherd, J. M. and W. A. Haslett's, S. P. Jones & Co.'s, and such grocery stores as E. T. Church & Co., bespeak enterprise and success rarely equaled in towns of the size of Charlotte. Messrs. G. W. & S. C. Sherwood are building, on the corner opposite the Phœnix House, a splendid brick block for a hotel, to be opened on May 1st, 1869. It will cost $20,000. The Charlotte *Republican*, a live weekly newspaper, edited by Mr. Saunders, is issued here.

There are two steam flouring mills, two steam lumber mills, three steam planing and turning mills, with shingle mills attached, and two foundries and machine shops, which make agricultural implements. The place is quite destitute of water power. Battle Creek, which is here a very small stream, runs along the margin of the town.

To Charlotte, Eaton, and all concerned, let me say : You are henceforth to enjoy facilities of locomotion and transportation second to none in the country. Your road is well officered and managed, and remarkably smooth for a new one. Your cars and coaches are first-class. You have the Great Michigan Central, with its unlimited facilities, its excellent management, its polite and efficient train officers, its magnificent coaches, and, especially, its splendid ladies' cars, placed at your disposal at your junction with it, and a few short and delightful hours' skipping along the " snow-bound " surface in the direction of sunset, brings you to the greatest city in the world ; the greatest for rapidity of growth ; the greatest for her success in surmounting obstacles ; the greatest for her energy and public spirit ; the greatest for her agricultural and commercial importance, and the greatest for her railway communications ; though not the greatest in mere numbers of population. She is metropolitan and she is your emporium. Her storehouses contain all that you produce, and everything that you consume. She is your natural, your *economical* market. Her accumulated wealth flows back on you in a thousand ways. Her prosperity, her greatness and her glory belong not alone to her, but to you, and the great Northwest.

Jobbing fifty millions of dry goods annually, and three hundred millions more of other merchandise, circumstances over which her sagacious merchants have no control make her your best market to purchase these commodities ; and do you seek a contiguous market for your wheat and wool, she offers it to you.

And now, commending Mr. H. P. Hall and his livery establishment to the *driving* world, I take Charlotte by the hand and say, farewell—

> " A word that must be and hath been
> A sound that makes us linger,—
> Yet, farewell."

X.

Michigan, December, 1868.

Editor Chicago Price Current:

Two hundred and eight miles from Chicago, on the Grand river, is situated the city of

JACKSON.

Like all other cities and towns on the Central, it is a hive of industry—a brilliant scene of refinement, activity, and rapid growth. Two hundred buildings have been erected during the year. The population is 12,000. The Jackson *Citizen*, a daily paper, has a circulation of 1,000, and is an ably conducted Republican journal. Ample banking facilities are furnished to the business community by two national, and an equal number of private banks. Large quantities of farm products find a market here.

Jackson is a railroad centre. The Grand River Valley, the Jackson, Lansing and Saginaw, and the Michigan Southern, intersect the Central here. Through the politeness of Mr. Bingham, agent of the State Prison, I was enabled to visit that institution, and witness the manner in which the convicts are employed; also to learn much that may interest the readers of the Price Current. The prison is undoubtedly the largest, if not the most remunerative, manufacturing establishment in the State. The walls of this den of striped apprentices to penal industry are 500 by 600 feet, and within them are quarters for seven hundred of these hardened " sons of evil." The present number of prisoners is six hundred and thirty, including a dozen women. Twenty-four of the prisoners are in solitary confinement, and the balance are at work on "the job." In the wagon shops are one hundred and twenty. The cigar factory, which is run by Messrs. Hollingsworth Bros. & Signor, employs fifty men. In the leather dressing and horse collar shop a hundred men are at work. There are also one hundred in the cabinet and agricultural tool shops. The remainder are at work in the other departments of the institution. Last year the prison ran behind about $5,000, but it is thought by Mr. Bingham that it will sustain itself this year.

Now on the Jackson, Lansing and Saginaw road, seated in a luxurious coach, Mr. E. A. Todd conductor, an hour and thirty minutes' ride over smooth rails brings me to the capital of Michigan.

LANSING

is thirty-seven miles from Jackson, and two hundred and forty-five miles from Chicago. With a prescience of her future growth, she has "spread herself," and will probably never be obliged to extend her present city limits. What she most needs just now is a street railway connecting the upper and lower towns, thus consolidating the elements of her strength. She has many beautiful buildings, and there is abundant evidence of increasing wealth and cultivated taste on every side. Of the public buildings the largest and most beautiful is the State Reform School building. It contains at present four hundred and fourteen boys, nine of whom declared their political preference for Gen. Grant, and all the rest voted for that other fellow.

The Lansing House, kept by Mr. M. Hudson, is a large and first-class hotel. Its dimensions are 120 and 140 feet front, with wings 70 feet each, and entertains two hundred and fifty guests. It was erected two years ago. There is an agricultural and a female college in the place. The Lansing *Republican* has a capital stock of $60,000, and employs one hundred hands. Last year there were issued from this office 240,000 books. There are many fine stores here; that of H. Ingersoll is one of the best in the State. The beautiful Grand River flows directly through the city, and a part of its glassy surface is fenced in for a skating park. All the world skates; why not the beaux and belles of Lansing? "All aboard!" The bell rings, and away we speed through the biting atmosphere, through the whirling snow, toward the north pole, and at respectable bedtime are shown to an elegant apartment in the Taylor House, at

SAGINAW CITY,

the principal feature of which is the beautiful and spacious hotel last named, built and kept by Hon. W. H. Taylor, than whom no man knows better "how to keep a hotel." Street cars pass the door every ten minutes, running to

EAST SAGINAW,

a most beautiful and wonderful little city. With a population of 15,000 she publishes two daily papers, one of them having a circulation of 3,000. The Saginaw river runs between the two cities. They are rivals. Saginaw City is *pining* away at a rate that encourages her citizens to believe that she will eventually become the larger of the two; yet East Saginaw is in such a prodigious *pickle* that no doubts are entertained that her ascendancy will be *preserved* to the latest day. However, that " destiny that shapes our ends " will ultimately unite the two Saginaws, and make one great city—the metropolis of the Wolverine State. Already their combined populations amount to 23,000. " Ye are the *salt* of the earth." From its manufacture, and 400,000,000 feet of lumber annually—the largest product of any point on the continent—Saginaw has an income of fourteen millions a year. Her gigantic resources and interests demand, and will soon secure, the improvement of the river, so that the largest vessels may pass into her harbor without delay or danger, and her railway communications are already adequate to her utmost need. The Jackson, Lansing and Saginaw is a splendidly managed public thoroughfare, and brings the Saginaw Valley seventy-five miles nearer Chicago than any other route.

XI.

MICHIGAN, December, 1868.

EDITOR CHICAGO PRICE CURRENT:

"Merry Christmas" descended upon me ere I had bid my adieu to lumber and salt, so substituting the "compliments of the season" for the sad phrase "good bye," I started back on the J. L., & S., and in a couple of hours landed at the National Hotel at

OWOSSO.

The National Hotel is kept by "Jake;" it is, *by Joe!* The National Hotel *beats* the nation; it does, by Jake!

Owosso is a thriving town of probably 2,500 inhabitants, situated on the Shiawassee, a stream of considerable size, which affords a fair water-power here, and finally empties into the Saginaw a short distance above Saginaw City. The Jackson, Lansing and Saginaw Railroad crosses the Detroit and Milwaukee at this point, but the arrangements are such as to seriously incommode the traveling public who wish to change cars, by a somewhat annoying and perhaps unnecessary delay of four to six hours. It could be wished that a change of time might be made by these roads, so that this detention would in the future be avoided.

The Owosso Woolen Mill, a new and substantial brick establishment, Messrs. Warren, Earl & Knill, proprietors, commenced operations on the 3d of September last. It has been running only one set of machinery, but has a capacity of three. The other two sets are soon to be put in motion. The average product of the mill since opening has been 700 yards per week. Cassimeres, satinets, flannels, blankets, and yarn, are manufactured, and compare favorably with the goods of any other Western mill. The 10-4 blankets are especially fine, made from Leicester wool four inches long, are combed but little, and weigh 9½ ℔s to the pair.

Through a rare atmosphere, under a bright and cheering winter sun, joyously and swiftly we glide along the D. & M., greeting Ovid with a "merry Christmas," and stop for the night at

ST. JOHN'S.

Whether the Evangelist, or the Revelator, I am unable to divine. Certainly there was no good news awaiting me; although the town is something of an apocalypse in its way. It is the county seat of Clinton county. With a population of 2,500, it publishes two weekly newspapers, has three hotels, plenty of stores, and is building an establishment for the manufacture of wooden ware and implements. The company is incorporated with a capital of $100,000. The surrounding country is said to be very fertile. But the hour for departure has arrived; so, "good bye, John"—St. John—and away we fly down the beautiful valley of the Grand River, through the frosted trees glittering in the morning sun, passing the picturesque town of Lyons *lying* on the left about a mile away, and are soon startled from our contemplation of the beautiful scenes all around us by the euphonious name of

IONIA.

She is a perfect love of a town. In summer, when arrayed in her trailing emerald robes, trimmed with the vine and the rose, she must be charming. Yet her beauty is not all masked by the ermine snow, and I gazed at her architecture, which is a combination of the Gothic and *Ionic*, with a peculiar pleasure; and her majestic heights, surmounted by those elegant mansions, were to me a delight and an inspiration. Soon a railroad from here to Lansing, thence to Battle Creek, will put her in direct communication with Chicago. Four thousand population and fourteen dry goods stores. "That's business."

On the road again, thundering along toward the lake, across bridges, through the forest, now among the hills, on the embankments, in the deep cut, on the broad plain, then by the river's edge, we go like the winds, and at sunset arrive at

GRAND RAPIDS.

Not quite; for the Detroit and Milwaukee road does not run to the Gypsum city. A branch—the city horse railway—connects with it at a place which we were told by a young lady was called "Dapo." After a ride of a mile and a half we were brought up *standing* to the city, which stands solid and stately upon her immense *plaster*, which is now *drawing* the attention of the fertilizing world. When the Kalamazoo, Allegan and Grand Rapids Railroad shall be completed, which will occur by the first of April next, a new era will dawn upon the business of the place. Grand Rapids will then be in direct communication at all seasons with the metropolis of the West, and facilities of the first-class will be afforded her for a more intimate business and social relationship with our great city. The benefits of a freer intercourse between the people of the two cities must, of course, be mutual; and while we need, and must have, her plaster, her lumber, and her furniture, we ought to, and can, supply her with her merchandise upon as favorable terms as she can obtain it elsewhere. We shall thus be developing each other's resources, and building each other up; and when the Garden City shall have achieved a growth of half a million of population, the eighteen thousand of the Gypsum City will have swollen to at least one-fifth that number. Chicago will soon hold Grand Rapids in her iron grasp, and it will be but another fulfillment of the "manifest destiny" of all Western towns.

The annual product of plaster here is 25,000 tons, and 300,000 barrels of stucco. The lumber sawed amounts to 25,000,000 feet annually. The hydraulic power is said to be the best in the State. The largest furniture factory in the United States is located here. There is a woolen mill and other manufacturing carried on. Two daily papers, enjoying a generous patronage, are in existence. The city has a delightful situation. The business portion of it is built on the plateau running back from

Grand River to the bluffs. The architecture is of the best, the materials being of brick or stone. In a few instances a plaster front may be seen, which is very beautiful, but not considered durable. The main street is compactly built up; many of the blocks are five, and some six stories high. A new and large hotel is nearly completed. The churches are especially beautiful in construction, and occupy the most delightful part of the city. The bluffs in the rear of the business part are a series of natural terraces, upon which are splendid residences of various styles of architecture. On the whole, Grand Rapids is a magnificent little city.

Strangers visiting here should not go away without calling on Mr. Albert S. Smith, manufacturer of gypsum ornaments. Every one, certainly, wants a specimen of plaster to carry home with him, and if he will call at the establishment of Mr. Smith, he can have it in a match box, a paper weight, a card dish, a goblet, a vase, a bracket, or in any article of use or ornament he can name.

XII.

MICHIGAN, January, 1869.

EDITOR CHICAGO PRICE CURRENT:

In a former letter we used the expression, "gentlemen's car," which seems rather odd, and may need a word of explanation.

Every traveler is familiar with the feminine gender of this phrase, and will readily comprehend it. Many great railway lines running out of Chicago are supplied with "ladies' cars," and it is but fair to our sex—and in this we think the *Sorosis* will agree with us—that we should have on every passenger train the counterpart to these: gentlemen's cars; cars into which ladies without husbands or escorts could not properly be admitted, and where woman certainly would be a little out of her sphere; coaches of the first class, furnished in luxurious style, with all the facilities for shortening the tedious hours of a long voyage, where the "tyrants" might retire from the

society of the "dear creatures" and consult with each other,
discuss the great question of female *suffering*, or color their
meerschaums. Now "smoking cars" are nothing new, but it
has remained for the Michigan Southern road to supply those
addicted to this manner of using the "weed" with superior
accommodations for regaling themselves. Gentlemen will
smoke occasionally, and they prefer not to be obliged to go into
a second-class car to indulge the habit; hence the Michigan
Southern has done well in providing genteel, comfortable, and
well ventilated coaches for them. While speaking of this road
let us add that the "coupler, buffer and platform," Miller's
patent, in use on this great thoroughfare, is one of the finest
improvements in modern railway affairs, making, as it does, a
continuous platform, so that passing from one car to another
when the train is in motion can be done without the slightest
danger of accident. Those going over this road will not fail to
notice this admirable improvement.

WHITE PIGEON,

the junction of the St. Joseph Valley Railroad, and a town of
about one thousand inhabitants, is one hundred and nineteen
miles from Chicago. The place possesses considerable interest,
is growing some, and its business, at present, exhibits some
degree of activity. Three miles north, on the St. J. V. R. R., is

CONSTANTINE.

Here the river St. Joseph is seen rolling placidly along.
Boats formerly ran up the river to this point. The town contains 2,500 inhabitants. There is a woolen mill, two flouring
mills, a foundry and machine shops, and a furniture factory
here. A union school edifice is being built, at a cost of $40,000.
Altogether, Constantine is an enterprising, active and beautiful
town.

STURGIS

is a lovely town. Its population is about 3,000. It claims to
be the largest town in St. Joseph county. Two weekly papers
are issued here. A foundry and cabinet factories are in operation, and a sash, door, and blind factory is to be erected. The

Indiana and Grand Traverse Railroad is graded from here about thirty miles south, and will probably be opened from Fort Wayne to Grand Rapids by July. This is now one of Michigan's most important public enterprises, and it is being prosecuted with vigor.

Twenty-four miles' ride down the Southern, under a clear sky and through a mild atmosphere, and we are in

COLDWATER,

which, at whatever degree of temperature, is preferable to being in *hot water*, and from all a stranger sees or hears, or even *feels*, on coming here, he will not be at a loss to comprehend why 6,000 human beings prefer being in Coldwater to being anywhere else. The city certainly is one of the most delightful in Michigan, and it can hardly be more pleasant for residence than it is profitable for business. On our *début* on Chicago street, our experiences were in many respects similar to those of a promenade in Chicago *city*. We were jostled by a crowd of well-to-do farmers; collided with an anxious-looking merchant rushing bankwards with a package of almighty dollars; squeezed through a throng of noisy speculators, and were so attracted by a bevy of bright-eyed Wolverines of the feminine persuasion that we stubbed the box-toes of our prodigious pontoons, and came near sprawling, and only escaped a serious *fall*, perhaps, by retiring to our room in the Southern Michigan House, whence we could look out and calmly contemplate the busy scene below, *sans* peril. The Coldwater river, a small stream, flows along the southern part of the city. The churches are numerous, very fine, and centrally located. There is a seminary in the place.

Two newspapers are published here. One of them, the *Republican*, circulates eighteen hundred copies, and is an excellent local and advertising paper. It is issued from an office supplied with all the modern improvements and facilities for doing first-class work. There is a woolen mill and a linseed oil factory here. The city burns gas. Its surroundings are rich in agricultural resources, and as a trading point it is unsurpassed by any town on the Southern road.

XIII:

MICHIGAN, January, 1869.

EDITOR CHICAGO PRICE CURRENT:

Leaving the pleasant portals of the Southern Michigan House, at Coldwater, an hour passes and we are snugly harbored at the Waverly, in the enterprising town of

JONESVILLE.

The place has a population of 2,000. It is situated on the head waters of the St. Joseph river, which is here a very small stream, scarcely affording power sufficient to drive an ordinary grist mill. The chief feature of the town is the extensive woolen mills of Messrs. H. R. Gardner & Co., so widely known in the Northwest. It is the largest establishment of the kind in Michigan. It employs five sets of machines and sixty-five hands, turning out an average of four hundred yards per day. Beauty of style, superiority of finish and quality, are the distinguishing characteristics of the products of these mills.

Four miles eastward we find

HILLSDALE,

A valley among the hills; a delightful town—built up in the most usbstantial and beautiful manner, and still rapidly growing. She is extending her main business street, and covering her picturesque hills all over with charming dwellings. Fourteen brick storehouses and a proportionate number of residences were elected last year. At present her population is 5,000. There is a commercial college in the place. Hillsdale College, an institution well and favorably known throughout the country, has a conspicuous and beautiful location in the northern section of the town.

Two weekly newspapers are published here. The Hillsdale *Standard* circulates 1,500 copies. Everything seems to be in a flourishing condition, although in business no extraordinary activity can exist at this season of the year.

We leave the charming atmosphere of Hillsdale with regret, and a ride of sixteen miles brings us to the beautiful town of

HUDSON,

which vies with Hillsdale in its charms. It contains 3,000 inhabitants. The business portion of the place is compact and presents a scene of rare attractiveness. The Tiffin river flows through the town and furnishes a fair water power. The place possesses some facilities for manufacturing. There is an extensive spoke and hub factory, and a cabinet factory here. A fine public hall has recently been completed. The Comstock House, a large and comfortable hotel, is one of the attractive features of the town. Two papers are published; churches and schools adorn and edify the place. The surroundings are fertile and productive.

Eighteen miles on the road and we enter the city of

ADRIAN,

the metropolis of Southern Michigan. Twelve thousand people, mingling in the scenes of busy life, in circumstances of wealth, luxury, refinement, energy and intelligence, form a political, social and moral power; and Adrian can boast of this number, perhaps more. Let her numerous and magnificent churches, with their lofty spires, proclaim her moral strength. Let her five splendid school edifices and her college speak of her intelligence and her purpose to diffuse education and knowledge. Let her stately storehouses and her beautiful dwellings show her wealth and taste. Let the rapidity of her growth tell of her energy, and let the manners of her people exhibit her refinement and hospitality.

INDIANA, January, 1869.

EDITOR CHICAGO PRICE CURRENT:

What with a meerschaum to suck, a harmonica to blow, and a luxurious chair in the *gentlemen's* car on the M. S. and N. I. R. R., our ride of fifty-eight miles on a frosty and radiant morning of one of the mildest January days, was one to be remembered for its exhilaration and its pleasure.

LA PORTE,

the door to Northern Indiana; a large door; a strong door ; a *beautiful* door. The door to agriculture; the door to commerce ; the door to manufactures; the door to wealth and refinement; the door to hospitality, with the latch string hanging out.

La Porte contains a population of 10,000. Kerosene and tallow furnished the "light of other days," and now Laporte burns gas.

A national bank and two private banks accommodate the business community. Two woolen factories, two large flouring mills, and two furniture factories are busily employed. A newspaper, the *Union and Herald*, pays weekly visits to the homes and firesides of 2,000 Hoosier farmers, mechanics and business men. A public library circulates its volumes among those who for knowledge are athirst, and a seminary is training the minds of the "coming man" and woman. Clear Lake, which is large enough to ripple, float a duck or freeze over, touches the northern limits of the city, and at present supplies the skaters with an excellent park on which to enjoy themselves. The Chicago, Cincinnati and Louisville Railroad, connecting with the Southern here, is completed as far south as Rochester.

La Porte is growing and improving. There are many large and beautiful stores in the city. Messrs. Davidson Brothers, have built and have occupied for about two months a very fine marble front double store, 40 by 90 feet, and four stories high. This intelligent and energetic firm appreciate the advantages of a near-by market, and accordingly purchase largely in Chicago.

Mr. P. King, another of the leading merchants of the place, has a large double store 46 by 80 feet in dimensions, and four sto-

3

ries in height. It is admirably arranged throughout, but the carpet room, on the second floor, is especially fine, and rarely equaled in the country.

Out of the rigors of business life there comes, unexpectedly sometimes, a genial, social element which in a degree, miti- gates the vexationsness of disappointed ambition. Those whose task it is to move the now stagnant waters of the business world, turn them into their accustomed channels, and cause them to surge and foam, and dash on to the great ocean of success and profitable transaction, will appreciate the affability and courtesy of such a business man as Mr. Julius Barnes, who, if not a merchant prince, is none the less the prince of politeness.

A sunken rock, or an iceberg, is a real and fearful obstacle in the channel before an unskilled navigator, while an " umbra- geous oak," casting its spectral shadow far into the stream, may, on a dark night, alarm him quite as much, but being too near it to turn his helm, in an agony of despair he lets go, and pre- sently is astonished to find that he had passed over the obstruc- tion unscathed, and that it was nothing but a shadow after all. In the stream of commerce are not many wrecks just now, though some are aground, and many more at anchor, or rather, becalmed. Now, it is very kind to a green navigator who is endeavoring to keep " agoing," and to create by his own *blow- ing* the impression among old mercantile mariners that a breeze is inflating their *sales*, we say it is kind in them to gracefully weigh anchor and haul out of his way, leaving the channel per- fectly clear to him.

And now taking leave of " mine host" of the Teegarden, we bid La Porte *au revoir*, and applying once more to the Southern for transportation, are whirled away toward the East, and in a jiffy reach the regal city of

SOUTH BEND,

eighty-six miles from Chicago, lying along, "high and dry," on the west bank of the lovely St. Joseph, is the home of Schuyler Colfax. The city contains at present about 10,000 inhabitants. It is clothed in beauty and throbbing with industry. With a capacity for manufacturing beyond calculation, it already has nine furniture factories, a wagon factory—almost, if not quite, as celebrated as Schuttler's—a pump factory, a clover machine, and a drill factory. A paper mill will shortly be erected, and woolen, and even cotton mills are talked of as possible within a few years. The Singer Manufacturing Company have put up a building of brick, 40 by 150 feet in dimensions, for the manufacture of their celebrated sewing machines, which will be in operation in a month hence. The Company intend to erect another building of the same dimensions. The whole will employ, when completed, two hundred and fifty hands. This Company employs in all its branches in the United States about 3,000 hands. Their capital stock is now five millions, all owned by the workingmen of the Company.

South Bend began to burn gas about a month ago. There is a workingman's library in the city. Two newspapers are published; one of them, the *St. Joseph Valley Register*, Mr. Colfax's old paper, has a circulation of two thousand. Indiana provides libraries for each township in the State, stocked with general reading matter. The number of volumes is proportioned to the population of the town. The number of volumes in the South Bend Library is seven hundred. Each family is allowed two volumes per week. This is an excellent system, and worthy to be adopted by other States in the Northwest.

The University of Notre Dame and St. Mary's Academy are about two miles from the city, and are patronized by both Catholics and Protestants, from all parts of the Union. The Dwight House, in its internal appointments, is one of the cosiest hotels it has been our good fortune to stop at for many a day. Its rooms are large, airy, and elegantly furnished. Not a thing is wanting to the convenience or comfort of the most fastidious guest, and the table is furnished with the best that the market affords. We remember the banquet of "Chapter twenty-nine," when the parlors and dining hall of this little hotel shone resplendant, and we forgot that we were not in one of the grandest hotels in the country.

MISHAWAKA,

is ninety miles from Chicago, and claims a population of 4,000
inhabitants. It, too, is on the St. Joseph river, and is a sprightly
and important town. There is considerable manufacturing
going on here. The place is growing quite rapidly, and there
are abundant signs of prosperity on every side. There are
several fine dry goods stores in the place, which seem to be
doing a fair trade for this season.

Eleven miles eastward we find

ELKHART,

with 4,000 population, a woolen factory, a paper mill, and two
weekly papers. The place seems to be an active trading point,
and has many large and elegant stores. The Elkhart river here
reinforces the St. Joseph with her waters, and the place enjoys
a first-class hydraulic power. The Air-Line road branches off
from the Michigan Southern at this point, while the main line, a
few miles further east, enters the State of Michigan.

THE CREDIT SYSTEM.

Before the Great Rebellion the Northwest was bankrupt. Two causes may be assigned for this, either of which might have been sufficient. First, she manufactured nothing; second, she bought every thing on credit. Her merchants procured their wares in a far-off market, and trusted them out to every body. Under such circumstances success was a miracle and failure the rule. The war came, and credit was refused. They found their way to Chicago, accepted our terms, paid cash for their goods, went into manufacturing, and began to make money. Peace came, and they, forgetting the lessons of the past, again demanded credit, obtained it, and again are languishing. Why? Because buying on time, though it does not *enable* the merchant to do so, invariably *induces* him to sell on the same terms. Grain, pork and beef may be his security; but suppose they are down, the holders of these products will not sell them, and he must wait. If they would sell at market value at harvest time—if farmers would keep their property moving, whether it was up or down, as the merchant must do, all would work well; but they will not: hence the merchant who sells them on credit must give them twice, and often thrice, the time he gets on his goods, or close his business and go into liquidation. Besides this, the system of procuring supplies of merchandise in a distant market turns the balance of exchange against us, and it is only a question of time when we shall again be in a bankrupt condition, if this ruinous policy be not abandoned.

Now let us look for a moment at the economical aspect of the question.

Were it not for the inevitable disaster that sooner or later overtakes the merchant who does business on the credit system, every Chicago jobber would be glad to avail himself of the

3*

immense profits which Eastern jobbers realize on their time goods. Every dealer knows that there is a difference of ten per cent. at least between cash and time prices. Let the Michigan merchant go East in February and buy his spring stock. On four months' he will purchase goods to supply his trade through March, April, May and June. It will take twenty days often to get his goods in store. Ten days after receipt of goods he may, if he is able, discount his bills, getting five per cent. off—still paying *five per cent.* more for the goods than if bought for cash. On the first of April he can buy the same goods of the same parties five per cent. lower than he bought them in February, in May five per cent. less than in April, and in June *ten* per cent. less than in May; but he has bought them in February, and cannot avail himself of the reduction. Perhaps his trade is dull, and he will have to carry some of them over to the next season, shop-worn, and with a year's interest added to the cost! Now it seems pretty clear from these figures that it makes a difference of twenty-five per cent. to the New York jobber, and in his favor, when he sells fancy goods on four months' time to the Western retailer. If the retailer would go to New York every thirty days, he might take advantage of the decline, but the distance and expense forbid this; yet there would remain the five per cent. additional for the privilege of having " four months" marked on the head of his bill, and there is no way to countervail this except to buy for cash.

Let no dealer imagine that because he has always discounted his bills he is an exception to the rule here laid down. He may continue to discount, and he may not. The terms of his contract do not require him to do so, and the shrewd jobber does not fail in making his prices to always provide for the contingency. The past season has been one in which the best of Western merchants have been unable to discount four months' bills; and the disastrous failure of the veteran house of Lathrop, Ludington & Co. is one of the unhappy results of such inability. Perhaps no four months' house in the United States is pecuniarily strong enough to run a single year, if the time were taken by all their customers, instead of anticipating their paper.

The credit system, however, is not absolutely ruinous. In the purchase of lands for agricultural pursuits it has been, and is, a great benefit to the individual and to the country. Why? Because *it stimulates the production of wealth*, and further, there can be no decline in the value of the soil of our country. Its appreciation is inevitable ; and, besides, from the enduring and immovable nature of this species of property, and the terms of its conveyance, it may be, and invariably is, mortgaged for the debt, thus securing the seller against any possibility of loss; but in sales of merchandise, or other personal property which is liable to fluctuation, where the title in fee usually passes from the seller to the buyer the moment the goods are delivered, *credit only stimulates the consumption of wealth*, and can be a benefit neither to the individual nor to the country at large.

COMMERCIAL INDEPENDENCE OF THE NORTHWEST.

The experience of the decade now just closing proves that the Northwest can manufacture its own domestic fabrics, and it should distribute from its great commercial centre the foreign goods it consumes. When the Pacific Railroad shall be opened, it will have superior facilities for doing so, and a new era will begin in this branch of commerce. The West must become a great commercial empire. She has every essential element, and the only question is, shall we pursue a policy that will develop our vast resources and secure at once our commercial independence, or shall we simply develop the resources of the soil, and leave our mineral wealth burrowed in the earth, and allow our powerful streams to go " unvexed to the sea?" Shall we continue to be all farmers and middlemen, dependent upon Eastern manufacturers and capitalists, or shall we be farmers, manufacturers, merchants, and capitalists ? Shall we continue to exchange the products of our eternal fields for the cotton and woolen fabrics we wear, or shall we make these at home, and sell the surplus of those for greenbacks or gold? *Corn is king*, and his throne is here. All the world acknowledges his sovereignty, and pays tribute to him. If that tribute cannot be paid in goods, it will be paid in gold. As soon as the Northwest shall comprehend this fact, she will act upon it, and henceforth her independence will be assured, and she will be imperial, for being endowed by nature with gifts surpassing all other parts of the world, when her resources shall be developed her aggrandizement will be supreme. She has the power now to cause the wealth of the world to flow into rather than out of her borders, and whatever policy will tend to permanently secure this ingress of riches should at once be adopted. If Western merchants will avail themselves of the obvious advantages which the great distributing city of Chicago offers them for obtaining their supplies, the point will be gained. The capital already here will be kept circulating in the community, and the entire profit will be enjoyed by the business of the West. In its increase it will build up our city, creating and enhancing the demand for every Western product. The tide of accumulating wealth will flow back on every town and hamlet ; it will open mines; it will discover coal-beds ; it will construct railways ; it will dig canals ; and it will unite the great lakes to the ocean. It will establish factories on every stream, and give employment to every idle hand. It will build churches, it will found colleges and schools, and diffuse learning throughout all its ramifications in the Northwest ; and while metropolitan Chicago rises up in majesty and splendor from the lake, as Venus rose from the sea, the neighboring towns and cities will form a string of pearls about her neck which must rise and fall with her every respiration. Proud of her gems she will be, and they in turn may feel proud of her, whose imperial beauty they will adorn and augment.

Among the Wolverines.